Dear Parent:

Your child's love of reading starts here!

Every child learns to read in a different way and at his or her own speed. Some go back and forth between reading levels and read favorite books again and again. Others read through each level in order. You can help your young reader improve and become more confident by encouraging his or her own interests and abilities. From books your child reads with you to the first books he or she reads alone, there are I Can Read Books for every stage of reading:

SHARED READING
Basic language, word repetition, and whimsical illustrations, ideal for sharing with your emergent reader

BEGINNING READING
Short sentences, familiar words, and simple concepts for children eager to read on their own

READING WITH HELP
Engaging stories, longer sentences, and language play for developing readers

READING ALONE
Complex plots, challenging vocabulary, and high-interest topics for the independent reader

I Can Read Books have introduced children to the joy of reading since 1957. Featuring award-winning authors and illustrators and a fabulous cast of beloved characters, I Can Read Books set the standard for beginning readers.

A lifetime of discovery begins with the magical words **"I Can Read!"**

Visit www.icanread.com for information
on enriching your child's reading experience.

Visit www.zonderkidz.com/icanread for more faith-based
I Can Read! titles from Zonderkidz.

When she opened [the basket], she saw the baby.
He was crying. She felt sorry for him.
"This is one of the Hebrew babies," she said.
—*Exodus 2:6*

ZONDERKIDZ

Baby Moses and the Princess
Copyright © 2009 by Zonderkidz.
All Rights Reserved. All Beginner's Bible copyrights and trademarks (including art, text, characters, etc.) are owned by Zondervan of Grand Rapids, MI.

An **I Can Read Book**

Requests for information should be addressed to:

Zondervan, 3900 *Sparks Drive SE, Grand Rapids, Michigan 49546*

Library of Congress Cataloging-in-Publication Data

Baby Moses and the princess / illustrated by Kelly Pulley.
     p. cm. — (I can read levels) (My first)
   ISBN 978-0-310-71767-6 (softcover)
   1. Moses (Biblical leader)—Childhood and youth—Juvenile literature. 2. Miriam (Biblical figure)—Juvenile literature. 3. Bible stories, English—O.T. Exodus. I. Pulley, Kelly.
  BS580.M6B225 2009
  222'.1209505—dc222   2008038604

All Scripture quotations, unless otherwise indicated are taken from the Holy Bible, *New International Reader's Version®, NIrV®.* Copyright © 1995, 1996, 1998, 2014 by Biblica, Inc.® Used by permission of Zondervan. All rights reserved worldwide. www.zondervan.com. The "NIrV" and "New International Reader's Version" are trademarks registered in the United States Patent and Trademark Office by Biblica, Inc.®

Art direction: Jody Langley

Baby Moses and the Princess

Pictures by Kelly Pulley

and Lisa Reed

Miriam lived with her family.

They lived in a land
with a mean king.

Miriam had a baby brother
named Moses.
Miriam loved her brother.

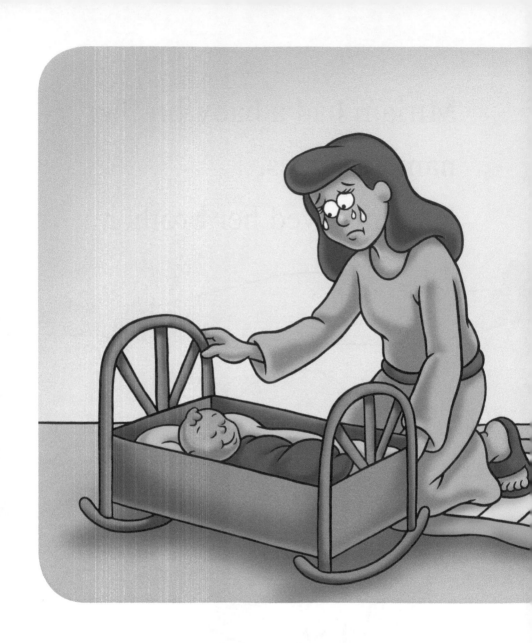

One day, Miriam saw
her mom crying.

"Why are you crying?"
Miriam asked.

"The king said he would
take away our baby boy,"
said her mother.

"We must hide Moses
to keep him safe,"
said her mom.

It was hard to keep
Moses a secret.

Sometimes he cried.

Miriam was afraid.

The king might hear Moses.

"God will take care of Moses,"
said Miriam's mother.

Miriam's mom made a basket
for baby Moses.

Miriam's mom put the basket
in the river.

She put Moses in the basket.

Miriam hid in the reeds
by the river.
She watched her brother.

"Please take care
of my brother,"
Miriam prayed to God.

The river rocked the basket.

Moses did not cry.

God watched over Moses.

Soon the king's daughter
came to the river.

The princess and her helpers
walked next to the river.
She pointed at the basket.

"What is in that basket?"
asked the princess.

"I will get the basket for you,"
said a helper.
Then Moses started crying.

The princess felt sorry
for the baby.
She rocked Moses.

Miriam watched the princess
and prayed.

"God, please keep Moses safe."

The princess said,
"What a cute baby boy!
I want to keep you."

Miriam ran to the princess.
"My mom can take care
of this baby for you."

The princess asked Miriam's mom
to take care of baby Moses.
Miriam and her mom were happy.

When Moses was older,
he went to the king's palace
to live with the princess.

That was God's plan.

God had more plans for Moses.
One day, Moses would save
God's people from the king.